seeing
beyond
depression

seeing beyond depression

jean vanier

Published in Great Britain in 2001 by
Society for Promoting Christian Knowledge
Holy Trinity Church
Marylebone Road
London NW1 4DU

Second impression 2002

First published in France in 1999 by
Le Livre Ouvert

The publishers wish to thank Allison Bell and
Diana Barran for their help in translating the text.

British Library Cataloguing-in-Publication Data

A catalogue record for this book is available from
the British Library

ISBN 0-281-05411-8

Typeset by Pioneer Associates, Perthshire
Printed in Great Britain by
The Cromwell Press, Trowbridge, Wiltshire

Contents

The human heart is
fragile
and vulnerable.

ONE

Depression: A Real Illness or a Wounded Heart?

I used to be a rather happy person by nature. I laughed a lot and I loved my husband. He loved me too, I thought. After the birth of our second child I felt more and more exhausted. Now, I find it very difficult to work at home. Everything seems like a mountain to me. I am more and more irritable with my husband and my children. I am even worried that my husband does not love me any more. It feels like I have lost all my zest for life.

Everything seemed to be going well at work. I was appreciated. Then my boss changed. The new one was tough on me, even unkind. I could not stand him, and it is true that I worked less and less well. Finally, I was sacked. Now I cry all the time. I find it hard to get out of bed in the morning. I feel like I cannot do anything worthwhile. I have lost all my self-confidence. When I look in the mirror I see myself as ugly. I am sure that I will never be able to get out of this hell.

Depression is an illness
that we cannot treat by ourselves.
We need help
to recover from it.

The human heart is fragile and vulnerable. As long as we feel loved as a unique person; as long as people seek out our company and find us attractive, amusing and intelligent; as long as we have a job, or activities which interest and fulfil us; life flows forth. We are full of energy and joy, and have a sense of being fully alive.

But when it seems that we are no longer attractive to others or that no one is interested in us, then we have the impression of being totally useless, pushed aside. Our heart is wounded. It is as if there is some dis-ease inside us; our heart is heavy and anxious. There is no more peace or joy, just a feeling of emptiness, a great inner void, which we try to fill by drinking alcohol, watching television or hyperactivity. We feel terribly lonely, and sink into a sort of apathy, overcome by sadness.

A new-born child attracts her parents' attention for a while. They love playing with their little one. But as the child grows up and develops physically, she can become less attractive; then as an adolescent she goes through a difficult time, becomes clumsy. The parents are less available, more taken up with their work; perhaps conflicts have begun to separate them. The child then feels less loved, less wanted. Her tender, vulnerable heart is

When our hearts
are wounded,
we lose interest in everything;
nothing
seems to help us.

wounded. She no longer feels important, precious, unique. She may even try to attract her parents' attention by doing stupid or naughty things, which only makes her parents angry. And the child feels even more rejected.

A young man was attracted to a girl. She responded positively to his glances and his gestures. They would go out together and seemed to get on well. They had the same tastes, the same interests and they liked doing the same things together. They began to fall in love.

Then, for some reason which he did not understand, she started to keep her distance from him. She found excuses not to go out with him. Then one day he saw her in the street with another man, laughing, happy and bubbling with life. He realized that she no longer loved him but was in love with someone else.

The young man's heart was broken. It was the first time he had ever opened his heart to a woman, the first time that he had dared to love. He was deeply hurt and no longer wanted to live, so he threw himself into his work, to going to the cinema and to drinking more. Anything to forget the inner pain.

The wounds
of the heart are
a normal
part of life.

During her engagement and the early part of her marriage, a young woman felt deeply loved by her husband. He would leave work early just to be with her more. They would go out and have fun together. He seemed so happy in her company! She herself blossomed as a result.

As time went by, he became more taken up with his work. He started coming home later and later. He was tired and no longer had the time nor the energy to talk with her or the children. He would just come home and collapse in front of the TV. She began to realize that his work was becoming more important than her. She realized too that she had lost some of her youthful beauty and was no longer attractive. She tried to open up to different activities but nothing really interested her. When our hearts are wounded, we lose interest in everything; nothing seems to help us.

A man who had had a successful career became unemployed. He started looking for a new job. But the days passed, without him finding anything. Bit by bit, he lost confidence in himself and his abilities. At home he kept busy, but he felt a sense of failure. He could not rid himself of the feeling that

When we feel loved
or admired
everything seems easy.
But when nobody
cares about us,
anguish
fills our hearts.

nobody wanted him and that he was no good at anything. He was plunged into discouragement and sadness. He felt lifeless.

Is this the same emptiness, only deeper, that a woman experiences when her husband is killed in an accident? They were united in love and in life. Suddenly he has disappeared, and the woman's heart is broken. She has lost all reason to live. She experiences not only her husband's death, but also her own inner death. She is in a state of grief.

When an activity or a person fills our lives, inspires us or gives us a zest for life, their absence can plunge us into this feeling of total emptiness. We live a kind of inner death. Life no longer flows forth in us. We are filled with a sense of loss and of grief; a heaviness, which resembles depression, permeates our whole being. This pain and this heaviness are not a sickness but a normal, natural reaction to a loss that touches the very meaning of our lives.

A person who has suffered this kind of grief needs time to rediscover gradually other reasons to live. With time and help, the man who lost his job may perhaps find another challenging activity. Hopefully the young man will meet another girl. The woman wounded by her husband's lack of love could maybe discover a deeper, spiritual life or new

In order to emerge
from this state
of loss and grief,
and begin a new life,
people need
not so much a therapist as
friends who are
prepared to walk
with them.

friends and new activities which would help her to emerge from the paralysis of sadness. The danger for people in that state of pain is that they refuse to seek help and withdraw into their sadness, seeing themselves as victims, constantly reaffirming that nothing and no one can help them.

In order to emerge from this state of loss and grief, and begin a new life, people need not so much a therapist as friends who are prepared to walk with them. These friends cannot nor should they try to take away the grief, but rather accept it with them. The grieving process has its own particular rhythm in each person. It needs time. We should not try and make it disappear quickly through artificial ways and distractions. Sometimes people need to cry, scream and shout their pain, anger and frustration in order to free themselves gradually from the pain and find new life.

But there is a deeper sadness that shows itself when a person feels frustrated or hurt, or when he or she experiences a setback, an emotional crisis, great tension, conflict, or grief which seems unbearable. The person feels overwhelmed by sadness; an inner death surges forth from the depths of their being. Life no longer flows forth in them or around them. All energy is sapped and all zest for life is lost. Initially this loss of energy resembles

Sometimes
people need to cry,
scream and shout
their pain,
anger and frustration
in order to free
themselves
gradually from the pain
and find new life.

the grieving process described above, but the depth of pain and sadness seems to be out of all proportion to the event which has prompted it. Furthermore, unlike in times of grief, the sadness does not ease with time or with new activity; on the contrary, inner paralysis seems to increase. The person feels that he/she is imprisoned in a world of darkness, completely cut off from others. Depression is an illness that we cannot treat by ourselves. We need help to recover from it.

Depression,
that dark and painful force
which invades the
deepest part of our being
and spreads throughout
our whole body,
has its origins in
the wounds
of our childhood.

TWO
Understanding Depression

Depression, that dark and painful force which invades the deepest part of our being and spreads throughout our whole body, has its origins in the wounds of our childhood that we have never wanted to own or to name. We have pushed them away into the hidden recesses of our minds, the unconscious self, wanting to forget or even deny them. But they can re-emerge at given moments into our consciousness, paralysing us with feelings of sadness, guilt and confusion. These wounds begin to sap all our energy or desire to do things; they can even make us want to disappear or die. Let us try to understand the origins of this shadowy area of our being, hidden deep within us.

The new-born baby is so small, fragile and vulnerable. She can't do anything by herself. If she feels alone, or she feels pain or needs something, all she can do is cry for help; she can withdraw and refuse to communicate or eat.

The beauty of children lies precisely in their fragility and their weakness. In order to live, they need to be protected, nourished and loved, especially by

To love someone
is to show
to them
their beauty,
their worth
and their importance.

their mother and father. If they feel loved, they are secure and peaceful; they smile, their eyes and whole body sparkle with joy; they respond to the love of their parents with love and trust.

But what happens if a child does not feel wanted, loved or appreciated? What happens if his mother is out all the time or if her thoughts are constantly elsewhere; if she is tired and depressed or too busy and preoccupied to respond to his cry; or if she responds with aggression and anger? What happens if she tries to possess the child, to keep him to herself, in order to fill her own inner emptiness, thus preventing him from becoming himself? What if the child senses conflicts around him, or if he witnesses violent scenes? He will be afraid, terribly afraid: he will feel alone and in anguish. Feeling neither loved nor respected in his own right, he will think that he is bad. It is because of that, he thinks, that he is either controlled to the point of suffocation, or at the other extreme rejected and unwanted, or that people are aggressive towards him. As a result he imagines terrible things. He thinks that he is at fault, the source of the trouble. So, he develops a negative self-image and terrible feelings of guilt; he feels guilty that he exists.

Some people think that children do not feel anything, that they do not suffer from the ambiguities

Broken relationships
create anxiety,
loneliness and
fear.

and contradictions of the adults living around them. But that is not true. Children have extremely vulnerable hearts. They need the truth and cannot tolerate injustice or lies. They have a vital need for their parents' love, tenderness and encouragement.

Loving someone does not simply mean doing things *for* them; it is much more profound. To love someone is to show to them their beauty, their worth and their importance; it is to understand them, understand their cries and their body language; it is to rejoice in their presence, spend time in their company and communicate with them. To love is to live a heart-to-heart relationship with another, giving to and receiving from each other.

Children suffer terribly when their thirst for this love and presence is not met or when this fundamental relationship is broken off without explanation; when others refuse to listen to them and to understand their needs; when they are deceived, cheated, mistreated, abused, or punished without good reason and made to believe that they are no good. All of this puts children in a state of confusion and anguish. Broken relationships create anxiety, loneliness and fear and a complete loss of self-confidence.

The pain is increased in their vulnerable heart by their own doubts and contradictions. They start to

Children can
become frightened
of their own
selves, of the
power of destruction
in them.

bear a grudge against their parents. Feelings of hate can rise up in them. These aggressive feelings frighten them even more and convince them that they are bad. Children can become frightened of their own selves, of the power of destruction in them; they discover the 'monster' within them. But how can they possibly feel hatred for their father or their mother who are their source of life, food and protection? How is it possible to both love and hate the same person, to want at the same time their life and their death, their presence and their absence?

All of this becomes too much for the child. The conflicting feelings, together with anxiety and guilt, are unbearable. He cannot understand them, conceptualize them nor verbalize them. These feelings put him into a state of confusion. He has to forget them, suppress them, hide them in an subconscious world, and put up a barrier between them and his consciousness. So the child starts to cut himself off from his emotions, which are too painful. If he can, he throws himself into a frenzy of activities, projects, games and distractions. He seeks his parents' admiration. He latches on to other things to forget and to be able to survive. But these suppressed feelings, contradictions and sufferings remain hidden in the deepest part of

Depression
is the result of
all these hidden sadnesses,
darkness,
and feelings
of guilt.

himself, in the memory of his inner being and heart. It is too difficult to face up to them, to admit to them or to express them. They form a carefully buried shadow area of guilt, sadness and hate. But in a secret, hidden way, this darkness governs the life and attitudes of the child as he grows up and will continue to do so throughout his whole life. It determines certain traits of his character and explains fears, anger, desires for power and other irrational attitudes. It also plays a part in determining his yearning for light and truth, for an ideal and for perfection which may be another way for him to try to escape the darkness and chaos within him, of which he may be quite unaware.

There are extreme situations of abuse, violence and insecurity that are totally unbearable for the child. But every child experiences some pain, even with the most loving, caring parents. It is so easy to wound a child's heart! Parents may be busy or preoccupied by other things; they cannot always be present and attentive to him. The child lives a kind of rejection; the deep personal relationship he had with his parents seems broken or shaken. He does not understand his parents' anger or irritability or indifference. Apparently anodyne words and gestures can cause deep wounds in the heart of the child. A world of darkness exists in each one, of a

Depression
is not
a shameful illness
that has
to be hidden from
ourselves and
others.

greater or lesser intensity depending on the sensitivity of the child and the pain he has experienced.

Depression is the result of all these hidden sadnesses, darkness, and feelings of guilt which have been buried deeply in the heart. When they rise to the surface of the consciousness, they can engulf one's whole being. These feelings often emerge with the death of a loved one or some other painful event, or when the barriers that we have built up around our heart start to crumble. All these dark feelings which the child had hidden or repressed are relived in times of depression, without the now grown-up adult being able to understand where they have come from. This impossibility of understanding why only makes the situation worse. Depression then becomes a shameful illness. 'I am mad. I must go and see a psychiatrist.' The person develops an even more wounded and shameful self-image; she feels even worse about herself; she feels excluded, abnormal, a burden to others.

The wounds of
the heart
are part of the
reality of life
and
cannot be prevented.

THREE

Chemical Changes in the Body

When a child loves and is loved, when he laughs with pleasure in the arms of his mother or father, his whole body opens up and relaxes; certain chemicals are released in the body. Conversely, when he experiences the anguish of rejection, fear and horrible nightmares, then other chemicals are released. His whole body becomes tense and contracts, his energy becomes blocked.

Our bodies are closely connected to our feelings. In many ways, biology and psychology are ONE, because the human being is ONE. Some people have a biological predisposition to depression inherited from their parents. Others, on the other hand, have a stronger constitution that seems to be better able to cope with psychological pain. Each one of us is very different, according to our own personal story, our family experiences and our bodily constitution inherited from our parents.

The terrible reality that some children live obliges them to put up solid barriers within themselves in order to protect themselves. However, they do not

Every human being
is a mixture of
light and darkness,
trust and fear,
love and hate.

sink into a depressive state, because their genetic make-up is more resistant. Other children seem to have lived an apparently happy family life: 'I was always loved by my parents.' Yet that does not mean that they have not suffered from unkind gestures, a lack of attention or some form of rejection, or from moments when their parents were unable to listen to them or offer them affection. These children may suffer from depression in later life if they have a physical predisposition to do so.

The wounds of the heart are part of the reality of life and cannot be prevented. Each child absorbs pain and buries it without being able to name it. This is how the subconscious self, and in part each one's personality, comes into being.

When some people reach adulthood they idealize their parents; they seem to have a desperate need to have 'perfect' parents. They have as much difficulty recognizing and accepting their parents' mistakes, injustices and weakness as they do their own. They refuse to recognize that every human being is a mixture of light and darkness, trust and fear, love and hate. None of us can escape this fact. All human growth is about learning to let the light penetrate more deeply into the shadow areas of our being; it is allowing trust and love to conquer fear, prejudice and hate; it is finding the inner

In each one of us,
there are these shadow areas,
this sadness and
depression
ready to emerge
at some level of intensity.

strength to live and accept our past just as it is, with its wounds, without escaping into a world of illusions and dreams. In each one of us, even though we do not want to acknowledge it, there are these shadow areas, this sadness and depression ready to emerge at some level of intensity.

We do not have
to become slaves
to these
feelings which rise
up in our
consciousness.

FOUR

Healing or Getting Back on our Feet?

These dark thoughts, which sometimes make us want to disappear or die, are reinforced when we find ourselves in the presence of people who seem to be living and advancing in life joyfully, without problems. The word 'depression' is frightening; we hardly dare name it.

How is it possible to help people who are experiencing this kind of suffering to discover that it is a natural phenomenon; that it is a necessary crisis which can, if well cared for, lead to a new inner freedom?

Depression is not a shameful illness that has to be hidden from ourselves and others. It is all right to suffer from it; it is part of our being and part of the story of our lives. But this does not mean that we should allow ourselves to sink into this morbid sadness. In order to find new life we have to react! We do not have to become slaves to these feelings which rise up in our consciousness, but we must learn to manage them so that we can gradually be liberated from them.

To be able to
put words
to the pain is the
beginning
of liberation.

Life is a succession of crises and moments when we have to rediscover who we are and what we really want. Women tend to talk about these difficulties more easily than men, who often say, 'everything is fine', even when signs indicate the opposite.

> What can we do for someone who seems to be in a state of crisis? First of all, we should leave them in peace, without asking too many questions. But the moment will come when we have to identify the cause of the conflict, to discern the source of the depression. Conflicts which are not named, or which cannot be shared, take on a disproportionate significance and depressions which are not expressed become unbearable. (Letter of Cardinal Danneels, Christmas 1988, p. 34)

It is important then to start recognizing the pain in ourselves or in another and our inability to express or share it.

Frequently the person who feels inferior, poor and broken does not dare express what she is experiencing. 'Nobody can understand me.' She feels guilty. She does not dare admit her weakness. It's as if she does not have the right to talk about her pain! She is frightened of not being heard or even listened to. 'Who could be interested in the pain I am living?' We are frightened of being judged or

Experiencing
deep grief
after a setback
is normal
and natural.

condemned, of frightening others and of being seen as 'mad'. So, instead of opening up and sharing our inner pain, we become even more imprisoned in ourselves and in our sadness and wounds.

There comes a time, however, when these block-ages and fears become so intolerable that we have to talk to someone we trust. To be able to put words to the pain is the beginning of liberation. If we are regarded and listened to with respect and compassion, this is an acknowledgement of our dignity and importance as a person: 'You are of value.' The clouds of depression begin to lift a little. 'I don't have a shameful illness.'

Sometimes we can find trustworthy people who have the time and the openness to listen to us; they don't judge us, or overdramatize events, nor do they take matters too lightly. This might be the family doctor, a priest or minister, a retired person, a friend or a member of our family. These people have experience and can help us, simply by listening to us, by taking our hand, by giving us confidence, by giving us wise and practical advice. They can help us to understand that experiencing deep grief after a setback is normal and natural. But it must be said that many people are unable to find anyone with this human experience and this ability to be a good listener. In fact, too many

She needs
to feel
that she is loved
just as she is.

people are frightened of listening to someone who is depressed. They are worried about creating a relationship of dependency; or else they just don't have the time . . .

It is also important to know if medical help is necessary and to distinguish between what is a deep sadness and sense of grief, which can be overcome with friendly support, and the inner struggles and depression which cannot be overcome without the help of a psychiatrist or psychologist. Depression can progressively lead to total closure: the person is no longer able to communicate, but is locked up in a prison of morbid thoughts. Unless the situation is this extreme, some general advice can be given: 'Don't judge yourself, don't condemn yourself because of these feelings of sadness. This is the lot of each and every human being. Let us try to understand the difficulty and where it is coming from and then to live with the inner pain.' A real friend, a good counsellor, knows how to respect depression. It is a natural phenomenon that has its own particular rhythm. We should not try and make a person emerge too quickly from it. She needs to feel that she is loved just as she is, and not only on condition that she comes out of it. It takes time to get back on one's feet!

Arise, my love, my fair one, and
come away;
for lo, the winter is past
and the rain is over and gone.
The flowers appear on the earth,
the time of singing has come
and the voice of the turtledove
is heard in our land.

FIVE

The Winters of Life Prepare the Way for Springtimes

We are all so impatient. We want *everything* and we want it *now*! We want happiness, fulfilment and life. It is normal to want such things. But we have to learn to respect the rhythm of our being. Look at the plants and animals, look at the vegetables and the fruit trees. It takes time to grow and to bear fruit. There are the summers of rich harvests, the autumns with rain and falling leaves, the grey and cold winters where life seems to have stopped and then there are springtimes when life is reborn. In the Bible we read:

> Arise, my love, my fair one, and come away;
> for lo, the winter is past
> and the rain is over and gone.
> The flowers appear on the earth,
> the time of singing has come
> and the voice of the turtledove is heard in
> our land.
>
> (Song of Solomon 2.10)

It is the same with human life. We are like the fruit trees. We have been planted in the earth of our

There are moments
of grief and disappointment
that are like rough
and painful
times of pruning so
that there
might be more life.

mother's being and we have grown. We were born, we developed in the sometimes rugged earth of our families. During our life, just as in the cycle of nature, seasons follow one another.

The trees and shrubs are beautiful. Nature is beautiful. Our universe is beautiful. In the Bible it is written that God looked at the universe with the sun, the moon, the rain, with the air, the earth, the sea, with all the plants, the flowers, the trees, with the fish, the insects and the animals and all sorts of birds. And God saw that it was good. And, at the heart of the universe, there is man and woman, and they too are very good. We human beings begin our journey on this earth like a little seed that is sown, sprouts, grows, gives fruit and then ages and disappears. This is the cycle of life.

Yes, each one of us with our bodies, our hearts, our minds, is beautiful. Each one of us has our own cycle of growth which brings with it ups and downs, summers and winters, good times and bad times; setbacks and times of drought are part of life. They are phases we have to go through, and a new start is always possible.

Sometimes there are also more radical, violent wounds. Death seems close. When we are hurt, we tend to close in on ourselves. It is winter. The

During our life,
just as in the cycle
of nature,
seasons follow
one another.

ground becomes hard. And sometimes winter lasts a long time.

Just as the vine has to be pruned in order to bear more fruit, so too each one of us has to be pruned. There are moments of grief and disappointment that are like rough and painful times of pruning so that there might be more life. But when it is winter and it is very cold, when the vine has been pruned, stripped of its branches, we find it difficult to believe that spring will come again and that life is lying dormant but will soon re-emerge.

Today, you are living
in winter;
trust that spring
will come.

SIX

You Are Part of a Beautiful Universe

You are not all alone. You are a part of this beautiful universe where each element has its place; each one is important. This world has existed for millions of years. The sun rises every morning and sets every evening. The stars shine brightly far above the clouds and the storms. They are so beautiful and so marvellously arranged! You are a part of this immense and marvellous universe. You are a man, a woman on a journey. It is true that today you may feel trapped by discouragement, invaded by sadness and by thoughts of death. It is winter. Get ready for spring! One of the differences between we human beings and animals is that animals are perfectly adapted to their environment. We can either accept or reject it, depending on our inner wounds and failures that have been imposed upon us. We can be open or closed up; we can say, 'yes' to life, and try to guide it in a healthy way, or we can say, 'no, it is too hard!' and even try to destroy it.

This 'yes' to life may initially be a passive 'yes', born of lassitude and of regrets, but it can gradually become a 'yes' of openness, of acceptance, a

Look at the sun
that shines,
the birds that sing
and the
stars that shine
at night.
You too are part of
this universe.

'yes' of joy. This 'yes' to life, which springs from the deepest part of us, is not a naïve or idealistic 'yes'; it is not saying yes to a dream or an illusion. It is a 'yes' to our deepest self, a 'yes' to our past, to our body, to our family, a 'yes' to our inner storms, our winters, our pain; a 'yes' also to the beauty of life, to the sunshine, to fresh air, to running water, to children's faces, to the song of birds. It is the 'yes' to our destiny and our growth. It is the 'yes' to our own true beauty, even if, at certain times, we cannot see it anymore. But it is a struggle to journey towards this total 'yes'. Today, you are living in winter; trust that spring will come. Tomorrow, buds will appear, then flowers and fruit. You are going through a bad period. Do not overdramatize things. Become a friend of time. Look at the sun that shines, the birds that sing and the stars that shine at night. You too are part of this universe; you too are growing and are called to bear fruit. Wait with patience. Growth takes time. Don't you realize that in nature there is no waste? It is only we human beings who produce and reject things without using or recycling them. It does not happen like that in nature. The leaves rot and become compost, which is used to sustain the new life which will appear. Even death itself gives life. We are part of the natural world where there is no waste, only the cycle of life and where death is continually transformed into life.

In order to open a door,
we need a key.
We need a key to
open the door
to life,
the door to liberation.

SEVEN

The Deepest Person Within Each One of Us

We human beings, men and women of the earth, are incredibly well made. In each one of us there is a secret part, our deepest self, which is made for sharing, heart-to-heart relationships and joy. But it is often hidden behind a more superficial part, made of feelings and imagination, of anger and hate, and sometimes of a desire for death. Sometimes the deepest self is hidden behind a carefully closed door, and we lose confidence in ourselves.

In order to open a door, we need a key. In order to open the door of our hearts and to discover the meaning and the rhythm of life, we need a key. We can let ourselves remain locked up in a prison of sadness and refuse to live. So we need a key to open the door to life, the door to liberation.

This key is trust: to trust that deeper than all the feelings of sadness and death, lies our hidden, true self, which is unique and important. It has a destiny, which is growth to the fullest life possible.

Do not let yourself
be overcome by
feelings of sorrow.
Have faith in the life
hidden within you.
Behind the
black clouds,
the sun is shining.

Do not let yourself be overcome by feelings of sorrow. Have faith in the life hidden within you. Behind the black clouds, the sun is shining. The key is this 'yes' to your deepest and most secret self, hidden behind the clouds of sadness.

The person with whom you accept to share your pain will help you, with gentleness and attentiveness, to discover this part of yourself, and will help you to love and appreciate it.

Instead of saying, 'I am no good. I can't do anything, I want to disappear and die,' you will learn, little by little, to say, 'I feel sad and I feel like dying, and I don't know where this is coming from.' So you gradually discover these two different parts within you: the secret, hidden self which is the source of your being and your life, and the other, wounded self, which sends messages of sadness, death and rejection to your consciousness.

If you light
a small candle in a
dark room,
everything is
lit up.

EIGHT

Struggling Against the Powers of Death

There is a struggle inside you between these two parts. It's as if from time to time your heart becomes a battlefield! The secret part, full of light, seems so small and weak in the face of the discouraging and morbid part, which seems enormous and overwhelming. However, if you light a small candle in a dark room, everything is lit up. It is a matter of trusting in this little light in the deepest part of your being which can gradually chase away the darkness.

The darkness may be pitch black and it may not be easy to light the candle. At times it may even seem impossible. Hope tells us, however, that life is stronger than death, light stronger than darkness, and love stronger than hate.

To the extent that you no longer identify yourself with your depression and that you distinguish between your deepest, real self and the feelings of sadness and guilt which well up, from you know not where, then you have the key to healing and resurrection.

Life is stronger
than death,
light stronger
than darkness,
and love stronger
than hate.

There will be struggles, sometimes quite fierce ones: on one side, your deepest self, hidden, starved for recognition, relationship and inner freedom; on the other, the powers of sadness, destruction and death which engulf you, which judge and condemn you, claiming that you are 'good at nothing', 'good for nothing', drawing you into a desire to disappear.

If you choose life, you will have to fight against this power of darkness. It will be as bitter as the struggle some people have against the grip of alcohol or drugs. But each time you choose life, each time that you trust your deepest self, the darkness recedes.

Do not let yourself be dominated and crushed by these negative feelings or by your negative self-image. You need to react against them. Do not put on a sorrowful face or dress in clothes of mourning. Put on light-coloured clothes and some perfume, take care of your body and do everything you can to fight against these forces of darkness. It is not an easy struggle, but it is worthwhile. It leads to liberation and to life.

During this struggle, you will be helped and supported by the friend with whom you can share and by times of rest and relaxation.

But at some
stage
we need to find
the courage
to stop.

NINE
Knowing How to Rest

There is a real danger, when these powers of sadness and inner emptiness, and the need to throw ourselves into feverish activity or kinds of entertainment, control us. We try to forget by keeping busy with no matter what. For as soon as we stop, the anguish creeps in and the guilt resurfaces. Admittedly, many people are able to keep going by doing that. They cannot stop, sometimes because of the necessity of life, but frequently because stopping seems too dangerous.

But at some stage we need to find the courage to stop: to rest, to look at life and to try to see where the pain is coming from. The dark feelings will certainly begin to rise up again and the inner emptiness will reappear. That can be very painful. We can try new ways to find peace of heart and a little tranquillity by doing simple, practical things: cooking, cleaning the house, visiting a friend, writing a letter, taking a walk, listening to gentle music, visiting a church, praying in silence, or playing with children. In the midst of all our weakness and pain, we can experience moments of peace and joy. We need to learn how to savour these moments of well-being: to breathe quietly, to let the warmth of

Little by little,
you will learn to
distinguish between
the ways of
peace and light
and the ways
of darkness.

the sun enter our bodies, to enjoy the company of a good friend, to let a hint of joy rise in our hearts. In the evening, before going to bed, to have a good bath and to relax and rest in the warm water.

Little by little, you will learn to distinguish between the ways of peace and light and the ways of darkness. If you want to live in light and peace, there are certain things and certain people to avoid; perhaps some so-called friends or neighbours who, because of their own anxieties or difficulties, create turmoil or distress in you. In the same way, certain television programmes or magazines can disturb you and bring up anguish. You will discover that your psyche, just like your body, needs certain types of nourishment, while other nourishments are like poison: they are harmful to you. They do not bring you life but rather turmoil. It is just like people who know that if they eat too much chocolate it will make them feel sick!

Thus, you will discover how fragile and vulnerable your life, your body and your heart really are. You cannot do just anything. You have to look after yourself and treat yourself gently, enjoying relaxation, relationships, peace and prayer which will help you to stay in the light.

Of course, you have to find a good balance. You must not become old before your time! It's not necessary to worry endlessly about your health

Learning to live is
knowing how to make
choices, opting
for that which helps
you live in peace
and communion,
and avoiding that which
worries and upsets
you.

when you are still young. Learning to live means finding this balance. It is knowing how to make choices, opting for that which helps you live in peace and communion, and avoiding that which worries and upsets you. This is one of the best way to fight the powers of darkness and depression. Sometimes the struggle is tough. You have to say 'no' to death and 'yes' to life over and over again. It is an act of faith!

All this may seem idealistic. Perhaps you have children who need to be fed and collected from school, a husband or a wife who is hard to please, or a difficult and demanding job. Each one of us has responsibilities and things that have to be done. We cannot always just go off on a holiday. And yet true inner freedom cannot be found unless the body is given time to rest. If our bodies and minds are tense and stressed, then the real work of liberation cannot happen. We all have to learn to let go of certain activities, to avoid hyperactivity and busyness. We need to learn how to stop, how to be, and to look gently at others and at the world and to receive a certain inner peace.

But in order to stop like that, we need help. A doctor can grant us sick leave or propose new calming medication, or our husband, wife or friend, seeing our exhaustion and stress may encourage us to stop and rest.

Never having been
expressed,
these feelings have
remained hidden
in the memory
of our body and
heart.

TEN

Going Down Into the Darkness

There comes a moment when, with the help of a competent psychologist, we maybe have to look more closely at the powers of darkness hidden within us. No longer can we run away from them, but we must try to discover their origin and why they have such a hold over us. If we are to find healing and inner peace we have to face up to the real questions, to put names to them. We must not let ourselves be overcome by feelings of unworthiness that bring us into a terrifying, imaginary world.

In this descent into this place of darkness, we have to be accompanied by someone who is competent. Otherwise, we won't have the strength to look at our shadow areas and to cope with them. They are too frightening! But with the help of drawings, dreams, through association of ideas and images, in gentle dialogue with a competent person, we will gradually connect with this world which up to then has been hidden from our consciousness. We will be able to bring into the open early, painful experiences that we have never been able to look at, and then begin to deal with them. If we keep

The more we accept
the truth in
ourselves, the more
we find the
courage to acknowledge
our mistakes and
our responsibilities.

running away from our inner 'monsters', they become bigger and assume a disproportionate size. But if we stop and name them and face up to them, they will shrink and reassume their just proportions. We no longer allow ourselves to be governed by them.

Our childhood fears and anguish will then begin to resurface: all that we went through when we were mistreated, abused or unfairly rejected, when we witnessed unbearable conflicts around us, which we thought were our fault. We could not express these awful, morbid feelings, feelings of hate towards our parents or ourselves, because we were so small. We concealed them at the bottom of our hearts. Never having been expressed, these feelings have remained hidden in the memory of our body and heart. They have gnawed away inside us, poisoning our whole being, condemning us and making us feel guilty. In order to survive, we had to forget them and hide them behind solid walls.

When we can put words to these events and past feelings, we discover that we were not responsible for everything that went wrong. We can be more objective, putting things and situations into their proper perspective. As we try to look at past experiences more truthfully, we demystify them. We

'You are unique
in my eyes
and
I love you.'

free ourselves from the 'monsters' and 'demons' that have exercised power over us, crushing life and making us feel guilty. The walls built around this inner world of darkness begin to diminish. And strangely enough, as anguish rises up in us, a new freedom also comes to birth. We discover more deeply the small, innocent, trusting child within us; we discover new life.

At the same time, with help, we may realize that if our parents acted as they did, with a lack of attention and thoughtfulness, even sometimes with a certain harshness, it is because they too were hurt by their own parents and by wounding experiences in their own lives. They are a part of this long chain of pain and violence that is passed on from generation to generation.

So often, a child who has been deeply wounded in his heart is made to feel guilty. And yet he is innocent and cannot defend himself nor understand. As he grows up, he can try to free himself from this burden of guilt by making others feel guilty for so-called faults, someone weaker, someone smaller. Thus, it goes on from generation to generation.

When we discover that if, during our childhood, our parents have hurt us, it was because they themselves had been hurt during their childhood,

The wounds of our
hearts then become
an invitation,
an urgent call,
to live in a relationship
of love and
unity with God and
with others.

or were in some way in difficulty or pain, then we begin to understand them better. We can then begin to forgive them. The past no longer has power over us.

Then, we begin to understand that we ourselves are not perfect either, and never will be! We too have our share in wrongdoing: we have wounded our parents, our children, our husband, our wife and our friends. When we realize this, we do not have to condemn ourselves, but rather learn to accept our poverty and inner brokenness. Then we can start to dialogue with others in a spirit of humility. We may be called to ask forgiveness from those we have hurt. The more we accept the truth in ourselves, the more we find the courage to acknowledge our mistakes and our responsibilities and to go forward peacefully towards the future, seeking out truth in everything; the truth which makes us free.

By opening ourselves up to the truth and to light in this way, we gradually discover the mystery hidden within our being and that we have been trying to run away from. If, in all things, we seek out light and love, understanding and sharing, if we do not condemn ourselves, we will be free. Depression will no longer have any power over us. We will be able to take our rightful place in the world. And

We discover more deeply
the small,
innocent,
trusting child within us;
we discover
new life.

perhaps we will sense the presence of the one who is at the source of the beauty around us and within us. In this inner peace, we may hear: 'You are unique in my eyes and I love you.' God introduces us to a communion of love with him: prayer. This communion of love is forgiveness and life.

This obviously does not resolve all our problems. Some wounds remain. But these wounds are not a punishment reflecting our guilt, faults or wrong-doings. They are the result of other wounds, which in turn were caused by still earlier ones. And we can learn how to manage them and to make use of them so that we live in greater truth. We do not have to hide them nor, of course, should we show them off, but rather try to see how they can help us to live in humility and truth, and how God is revealed to us in and through them. The wounds of our hearts then become an invitation, an urgent call, to live in a relationship of love and unity with God and with others.

Depression is a
painful reality, a crisis,
but at the
same time crisis
can bring us to greater
freedom
if we discover how
to live with it
and how to move
towards healing.

ELEVEN

Depression: A Crisis Which Can Set Us Free

Depression is a painful reality, a crisis, but at the same time crisis can bring us to greater freedom if we discover how to live with it and how to move towards healing.

Depression, such as we have described, is the emergence in our consciousness of a hidden pain that has its origin in our early childhood. These hidden sufferings determine many of our attitudes, even if we are not aware of it. They prevent us from being free. They are like a huge weight on our hearts, a poison in our blood. Then one day, we become more aware, terribly aware of this inner pain and it is like an infection that turns into an abscess. We can then name the 'dis-ease', and seek its origins, and the way towards healing.

When depression becomes more visible, better accepted as such, it can lead us towards a genuine liberation of the heart. It obliges us to stop and look at what is really important in our own lives and in life in general. It puts us in touch with our deepest need, the need for love and a communion

When depression
becomes more visible,
it can lead us
towards a genuine
liberation
of the heart.

of hearts, but also with our fears of them. It helps us to see that, above and beyond all human relationships, it is possible for us to drink from the source of the universe and of life.

Other aspects to be considered

For some people, the descent into their inner darkness is so painful that they need medication in order to do it. The anguish is too powerful. Medication can not only calm the inner distress and allow them to continue on with daily life, but it can also restore to the body those substances which have been 'eaten up' by the depression. Constant tiredness, complete exhaustion and lack of energy often accompany depression; it can even be difficult to get out of bed in the morning!

This fatigue comes from the depression, but a good doctor will also do a physical check-up to see if the person is anaemic or lacking in vitamins or other basic substances. They might need some vitamins or minerals. A dietitian can also help to find the appropriate diet. The right food and the extra vitamins can supply the necessary energy to combat depression and so prevent it from overwhelming the person. They can help him/her to do and to discover new things, different activities

Our universe is not
made up only
of beautiful trees,
but also of stunted ones.
Yet each tree
is important.

and to become free from the power of darkness which paralyses them.

Each one of us is both body and spirit. Each one has his/her own physical make-up, psychological history and spiritual journey. We are one person. However, we risk becoming fragmented within ourselves and allowing divisions to become rooted in us. It is not just the pain of our past lives that prevents us from being fully alive and restricts us in sadness; it is also our refusal to look at and accept reality, to live in the truth of who we are and to take responsibility for our own lives.

We cannot be men and women fully alive if we reject life, if we refuse to accept reality, events and people around us just as they are; if we live in lies, illusions or prejudices; if we live in corruption and destroy the lives of others by the sale of drugs, or if we oppress or abuse others, we cannot be happy. It is as if we have become locked up in ourselves, in our own need for power and pleasure; we seem to be unable to see others as people who also have their desires and needs.

By refusing to see others as truly human, we also refuse to see ourselves as truly human. By rejecting life in others, we reject life within our own being. If we try to free ourselves from depression through

We fight against
depression
in order to live
and to give
life to others.

therapy and then close ourselves up in a prison of selfishness, that is another form of death. If we want to free ourselves from the consequences of the pain and oppression of our childhood, it cannot be so that we can oppress other people! We fight against depression in order to live and to give life to others. And when we start to live more fully we discover a meaning to our life.

To get out of depression,
which is a kind of
imprisonment,
first of all we must want
to do so.
We also need a good
therapist and,
even more important,
a network of friends who
love and accept us.

TWELVE
Getting Out of Depression

To get out of depression, which is a kind of imprisonment, first of all we must *want* to do so. We also need a good therapist and, even more important, a network of friends who love and accept us. They will sustain us in difficult moments, when we feel particularly fragile; depression can make us feel so very vulnerable. The slightest setback or sense of rejection, or a traumatic event, can nourish or revive our sense of powerlessness. Friends can help us to walk through the pain.

Friends are sometimes unable, however, to understand the depth of our pain, the 'hell' we are living. They might think they do, but we know that they do not! Parker Palmer, who went through a deep depression, wrote of how he felt blocked off from many friends who came to see him and told him 'nice thoughts'. He was lonely, terribly lonely, locked up in pain. There was one person, however, who came for just a quarter of an hour each day to massage his feet, without saying too much. This person helped Parker Palmer the most when one day he told him, 'I feel you are a little bit stronger today'.* Friends are called to walk with those in depression and not to make glib remarks.

They do not live any more
in a world of dreams
or illusions,
in anger or despair.
They no longer feel they
have to be other
then who they are.
They have the right to
be themselves.
And they discover that
they are loved by God,
precious in his eyes.

Some people may be helped by sessions of therapy, but a certain fragility remains with them. They have to continue to take medication. They may have to be hospitalized again. All that can be very painful for them. The presence of friends who accept them as they are, who do not give them inappropriate advice, can be a tremendous help, but such friendships do not necessarily prevent setbacks. People who have known times of depression can live in fear, anxiously waiting for the slightest sign of a relapse.

It takes time to accept the cycle of fragility and depression. It takes time to come to terms with reality. But when a person does, the results are amazing. He or she can discover their mission in life. Often the greatest support for people who have been hospitalized comes from other patients; their understanding, kindness and friendship are all factors in the healing process. Isn't it people who have known the weakness and pain of alcoholism who can help others in the same situation? That is the basic vision of Alcoholics Anonymous. Each person has to discover his/her fragility and handicap. Each one has to learn how to 'own' it, live with it and not let it control his/her life. Each person has to discover the meaning of their lives, the meaning of their brokenness and weakness.

The beauty of
human beings lies in
their capacity
to accept who
they are.

People who have suffered seem to understand much better the pain of other people.

Our universe is not made up only of beautiful trees, but also of stunted ones. Yet each tree is important. Television shows us movie stars, men and women with beautiful bodies and extravagant clothes. But that is not the reality of the majority of people! Each person is a mixture of gifts and fragilities. For some this fragility is physical; they are limited in their physical capacities and have to be careful of what they do and eat. Others are psychologically fragile because of an accident, or failure in life, or grief and loss. Other people's fragility comes from abandonment or abuse in their early childhood. A great number of people in shanty towns and slum areas, or in the Third World know the fragility and insecurity of economic poverty or the effects of war and conflict; many are refugees. Each person carries within himself/herself both strength and weakness, gifts and pain.

The beauty of human beings lies in their capacity to accept who they are, just as they are; not to live in a world of dreams or illusions, in anger or despair, wanting to be other than they are, or trying to run away from reality. They realize that they have the right to be themselves. And there, they discover that they are loved by God, that they are unique

We are all called to
love and be loved,
wherever we may be.
We are called
to be open and grow
in love and
thus to communicate
life to others.

and important for God and that they can do things for others. We may not all be called to do great things that make the headlines, but we are all called to love and be loved, wherever we may be. We are called to be open and to grow in love and thus to communicate life to others, especially to those in need.

*Parker Palmer, '"All the Way Down": Depression and the Spiritual Journey', in *Weavings* 13, Sept/Oct 1998, pp. 31–41.